AF480920

TRACING SHAPES FOR PREWRITING SKILLS

Writing Book Preschool
Children's Reading & Writing Books

Speedy Publishing LLC
40 E. Main St. #1156
Newark, DE 19711
www.speedypublishing.com

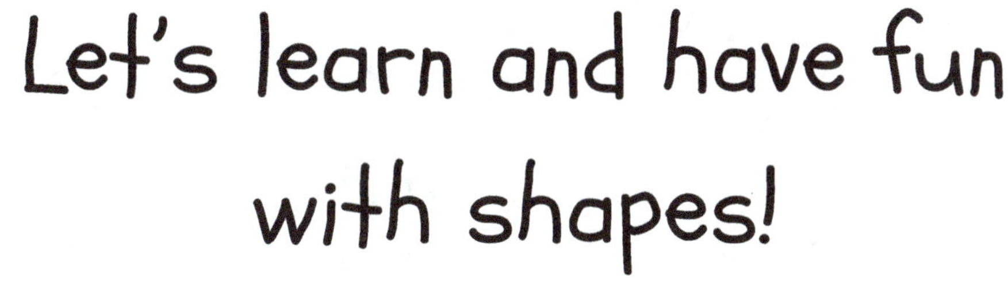

Let's learn and have fun with shapes!

Let's Learn SHAPES

CIRCLE

SQUARE

TRIANGLE

HEXAGON

RECTANGLE

CROSS

PENTAGON

TRAPEZIUM

ARROW
HEART
STAR
DIAMOND
QUATREFOIL
OVAL
PARALLELOGRAM
OCTAGON

It's your turn to practice tracing shapes! Let's have some tracing warm up first.

PRACTICE YOUR HANDWRITING BY TRACING THE FOLLOWING.

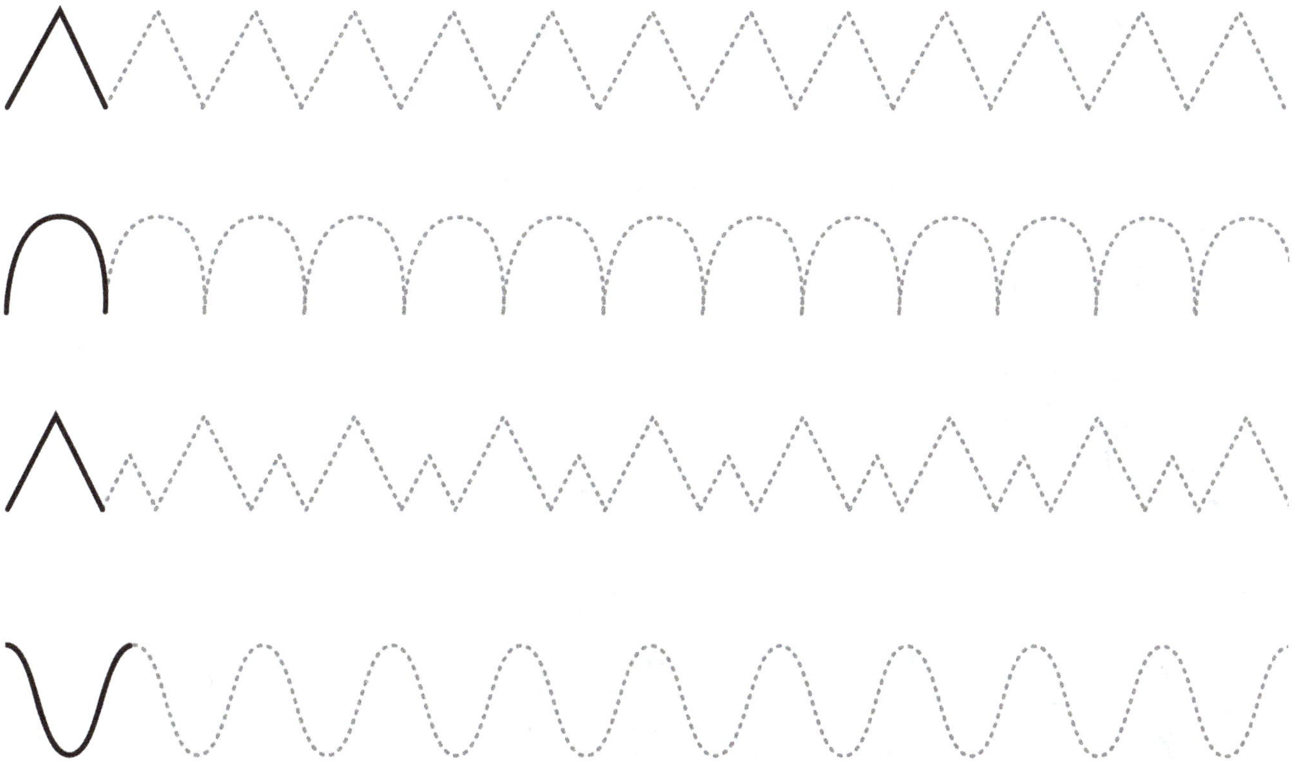

PRACTICE YOUR HANDWRITING BY TRACING THE FOLLOWING.

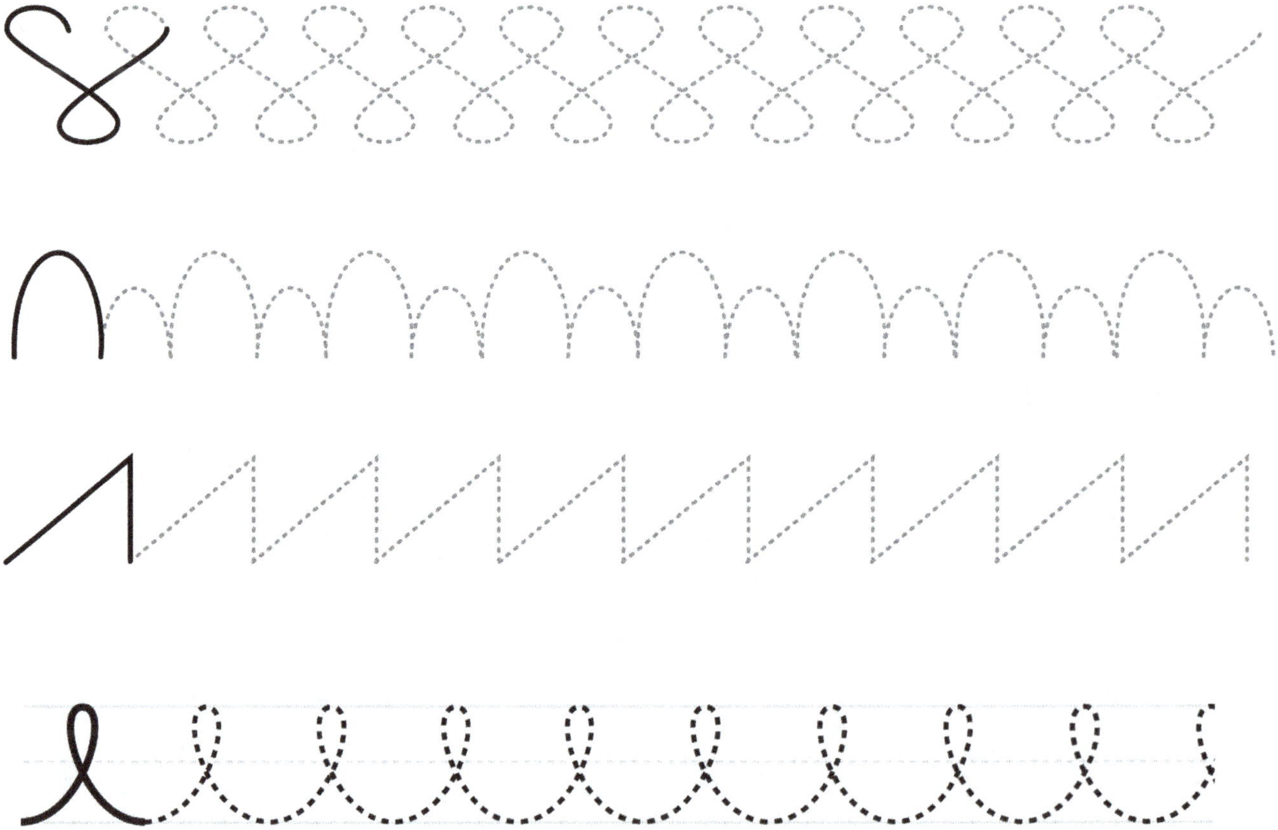

PRACTICE YOUR HANDWRITING BY TRACING THE FOLLOWING.

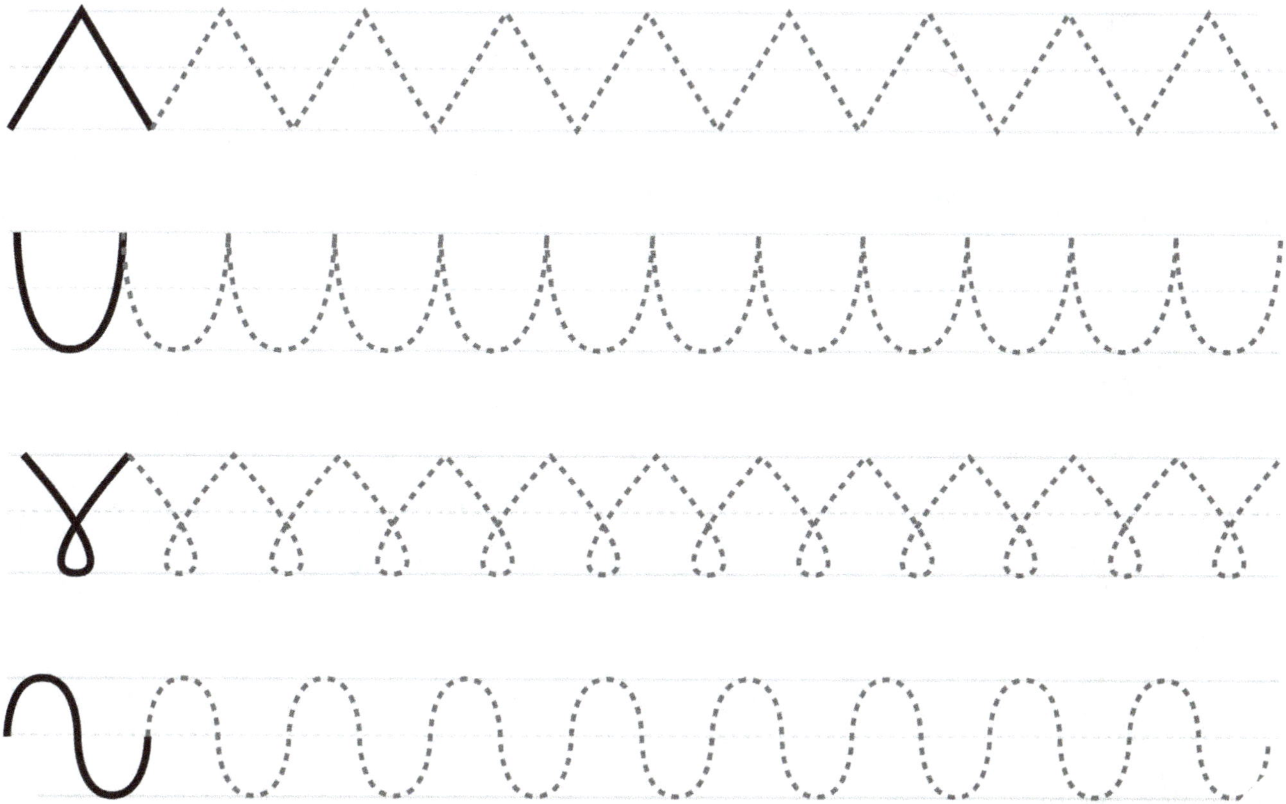

PRACTICE YOUR HANDWRITING BY TRACING THE FOLLOWING.

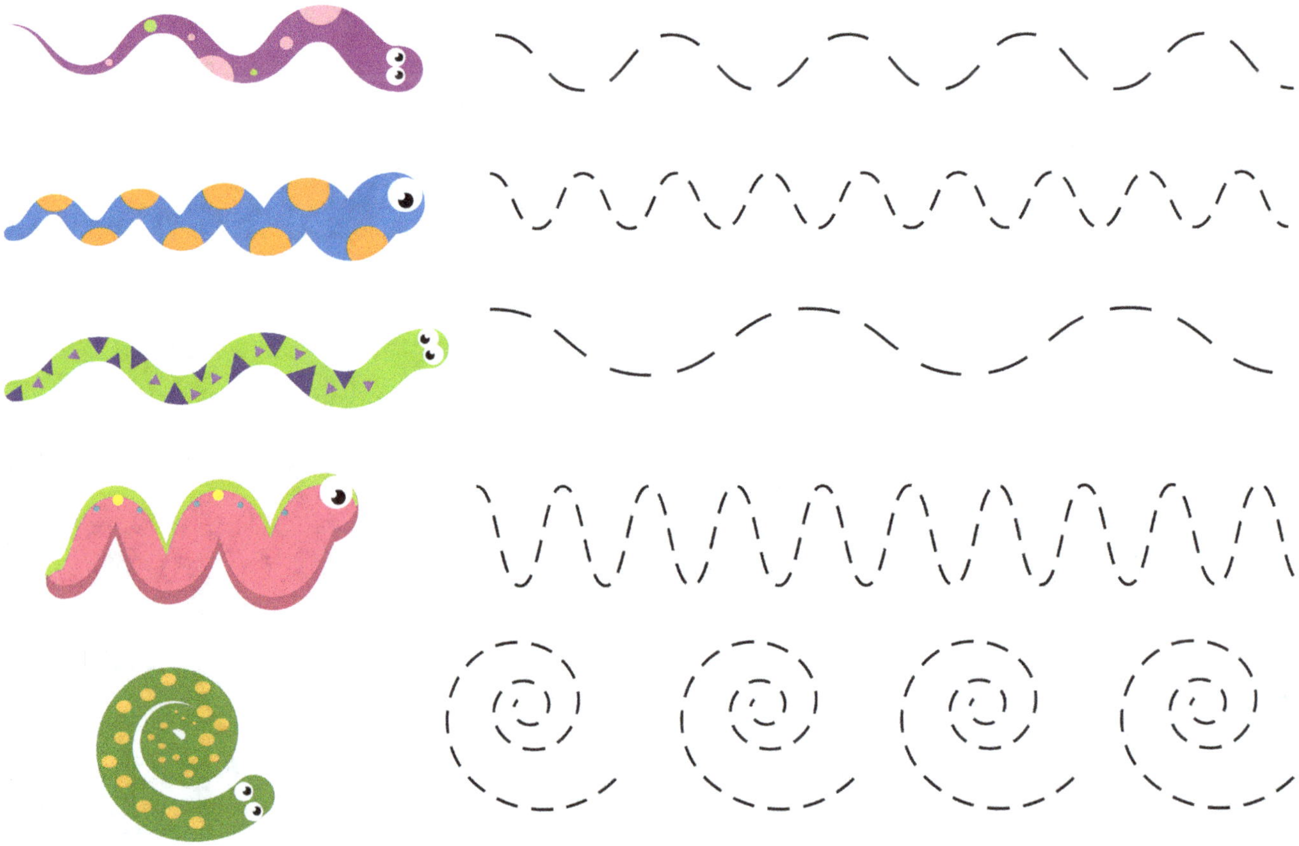

PRACTICE YOUR HANDWRITING BY TRACING THE FOLLOWING.

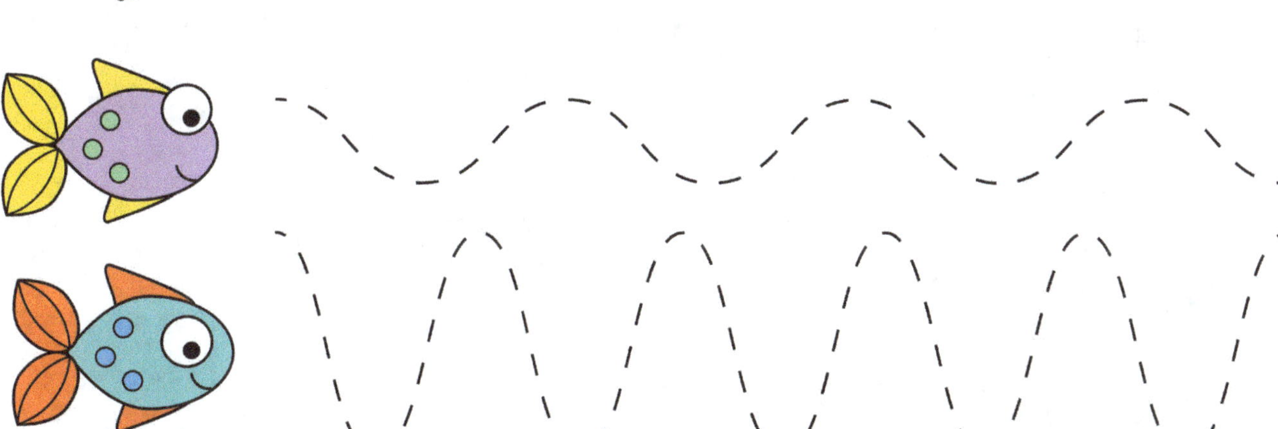

PRACTICE YOUR HANDWRITING BY TRACING THE FOLLOWING.

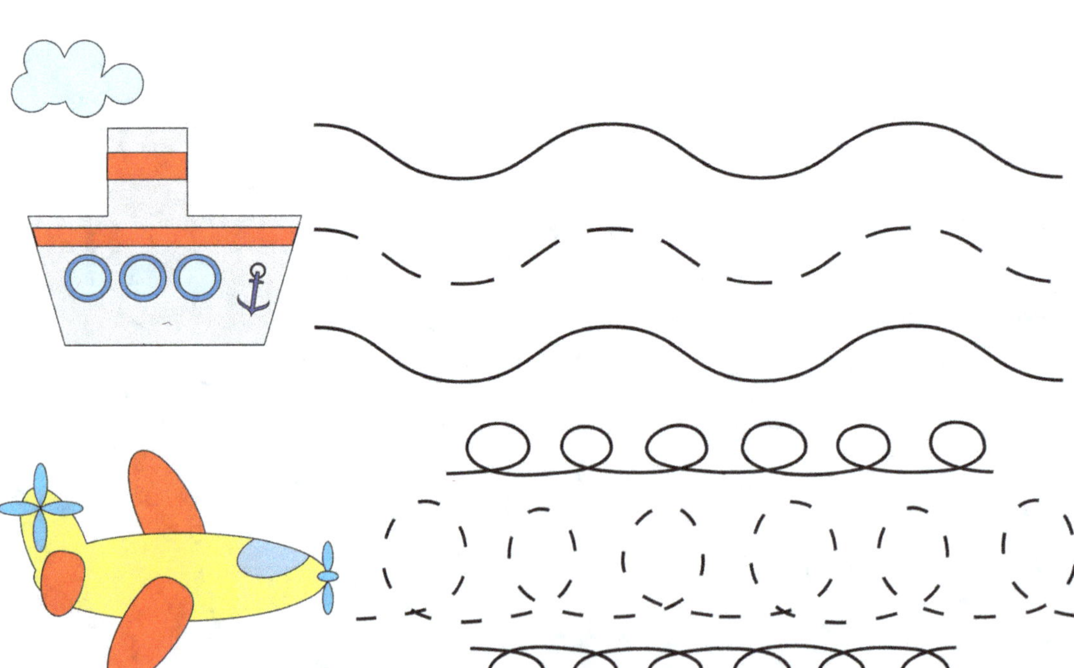

PRACTICE YOUR HANDWRITING BY TRACING THE FOLLOWING.

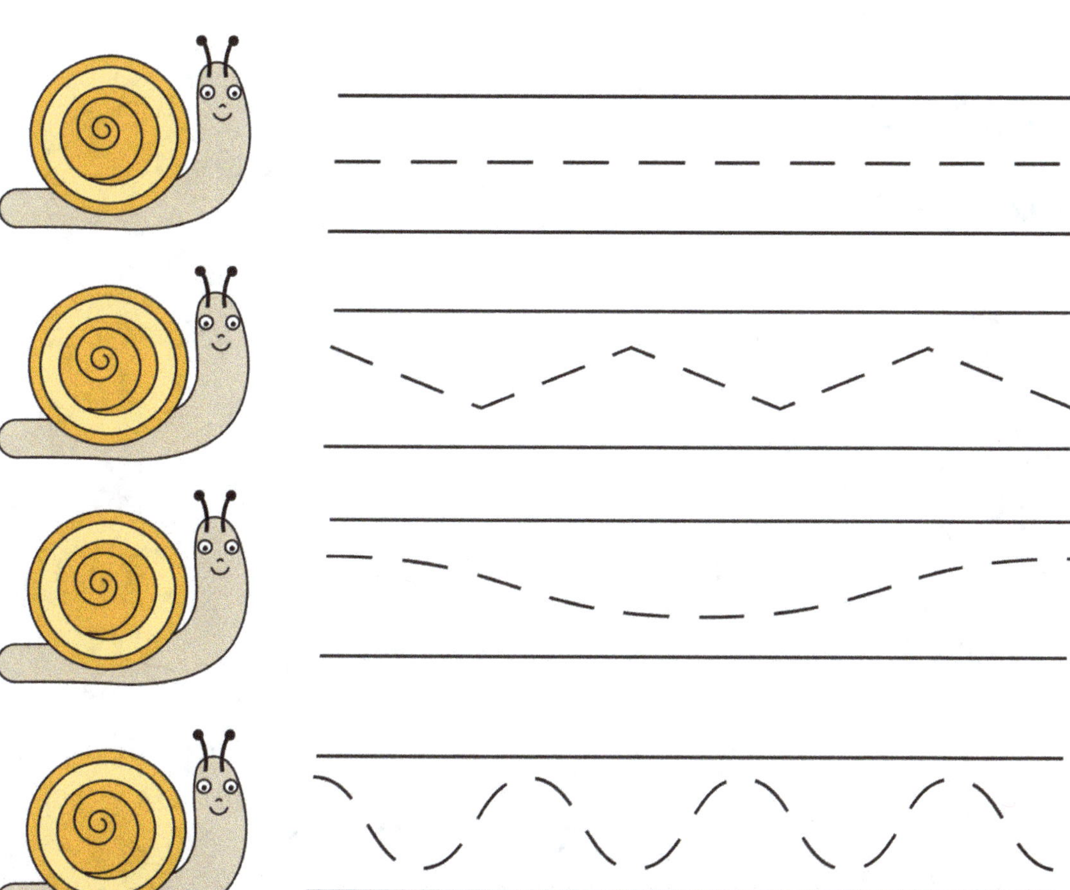

PRACTICE YOUR HANDWRITING BY TRACING THE FOLLOWING.

Let's trace the shapes!

TRACE THE SHAPE.

TRACE THE SHAPE.

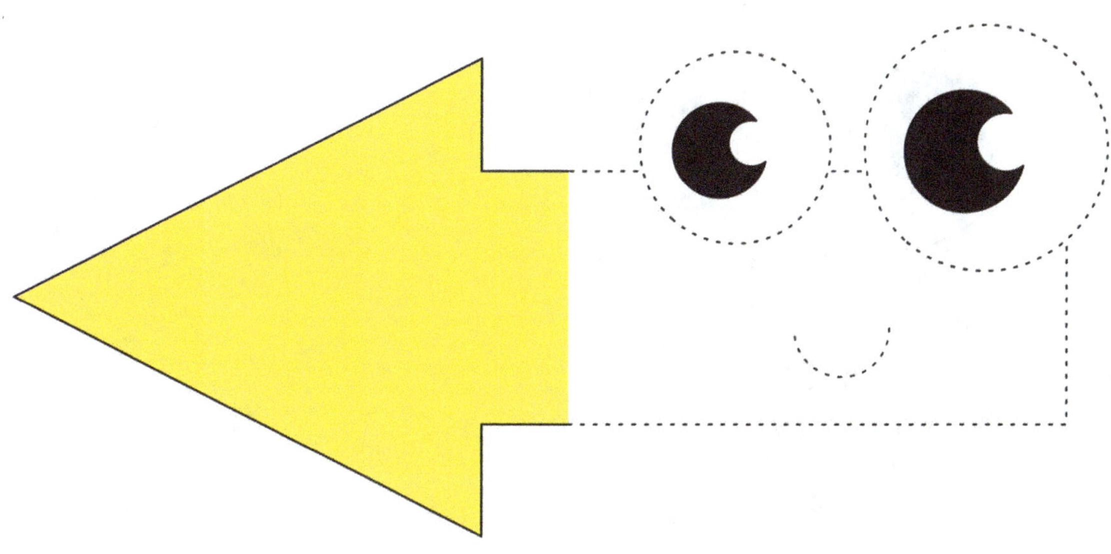

TRACE THE SHAPE.

TRACE THE SHAPE.

TRACE THE SHAPE.

TRACE THE SHAPE.

TRACE THE SHAPE.

TRACE THE SHAPE.

TRACE THE SHAPE.

TRACE THE SHAPE.

TRACE THE SHAPE.

TRACE THE SHAPE.

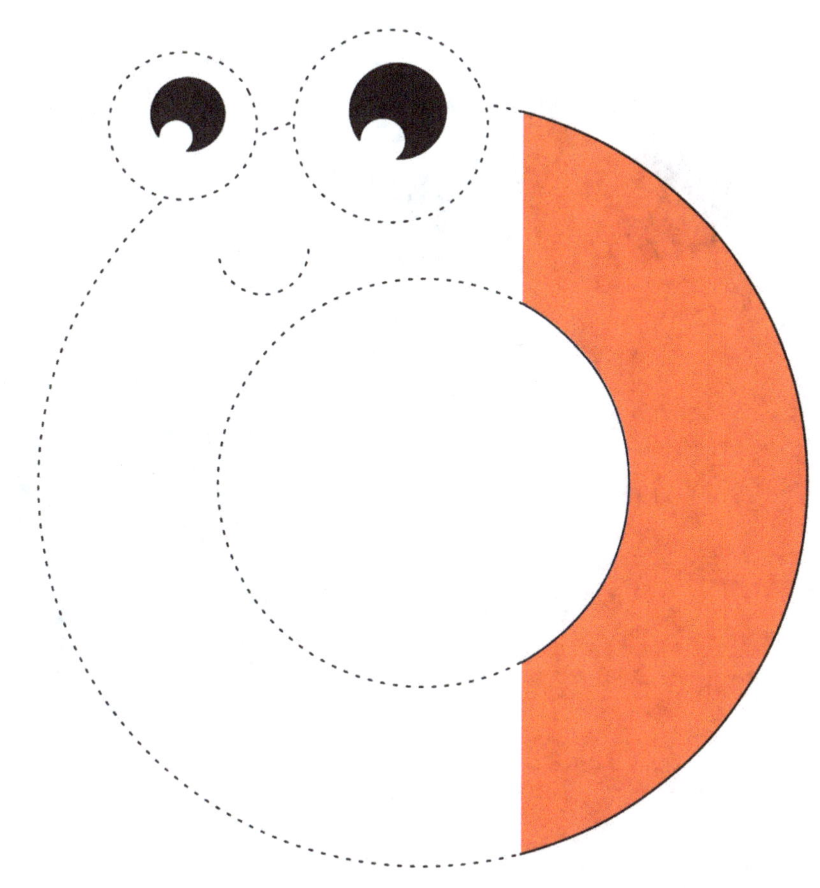

TRACE THE SHAPE.

TRACE THE SHAPE.

TRACE THE SHAPE.

TRACE THE SHAPE.

TRACE THE SHAPE.

Let's practice staying in the lines with these next exercises!

DRAW A LINE TO CONNECT THE SHAPE AND FORM A SHAPE.

DRAW A LINE TO CONNECT THE SHAPE AND FORM A SHAPE.

DRAW A LINE TO CONNECT THE SHAPE AND FORM A SHAPE.

DRAW A LINE TO CONNECT THE SHAPE AND FORM A SHAPE.

DRAW A LINE TO CONNECT THE SHAPE AND FORM A SHAPE.

DRAW A LINE TO CONNECT THE SHAPE AND FORM A SHAPE.

DRAW A LINE TO CONNECT THE SHAPE AND FORM A SHAPE.

DRAW A LINE TO CONNECT THE SHAPE AND FORM A SHAPE.

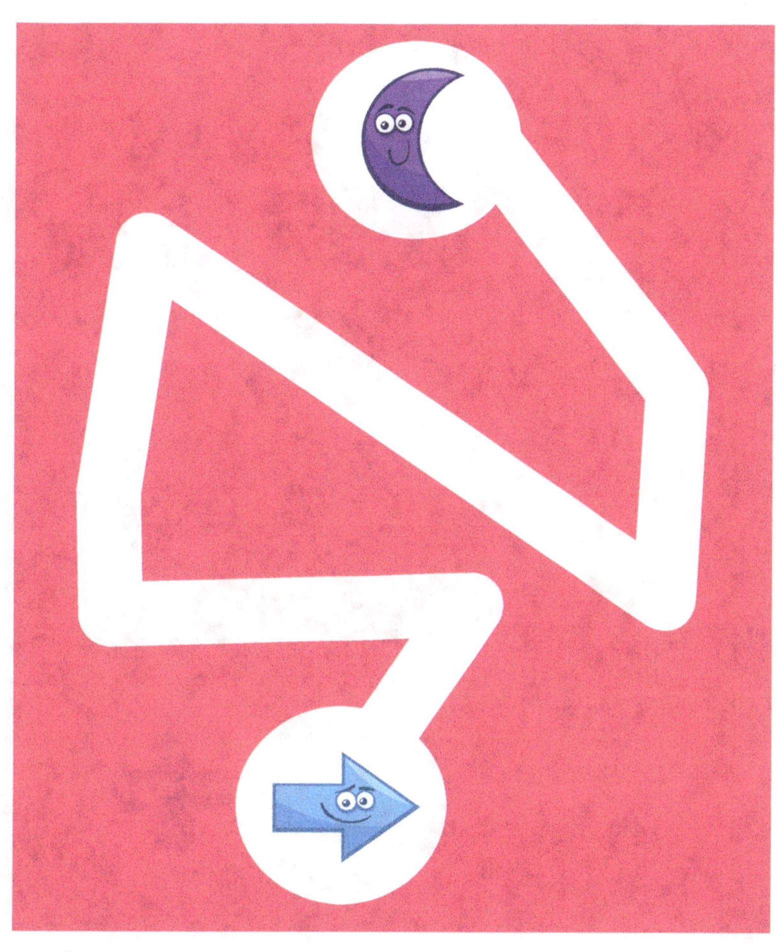

DRAW A LINE TO CONNECT THE SHAPE AND FORM A SHAPE.

DRAW A LINE TO CONNECT THE SHAPE AND FORM A SHAPE.

DRAW A LINE TO CONNECT THE SHAPE AND FORM A SHAPE.

DRAW A LINE TO CONNECT THE SHAPE AND FORM A SHAPE.

DRAW A LINE TO CONNECT THE SHAPE AND FORM A SHAPE.

DRAW A LINE TO CONNECT THE SHAPE AND FORM A SHAPE.

DRAW A LINE TO CONNECT THE SHAPE AND FORM A SHAPE.

DRAW A LINE TO CONNECT THE SHAPE AND FORM A SHAPE.

DRAW A LINE TO CONNECT THE SHAPE AND FORM A SHAPE.

DRAW A LINE TO CONNECT THE SHAPE AND FORM A SHAPE.

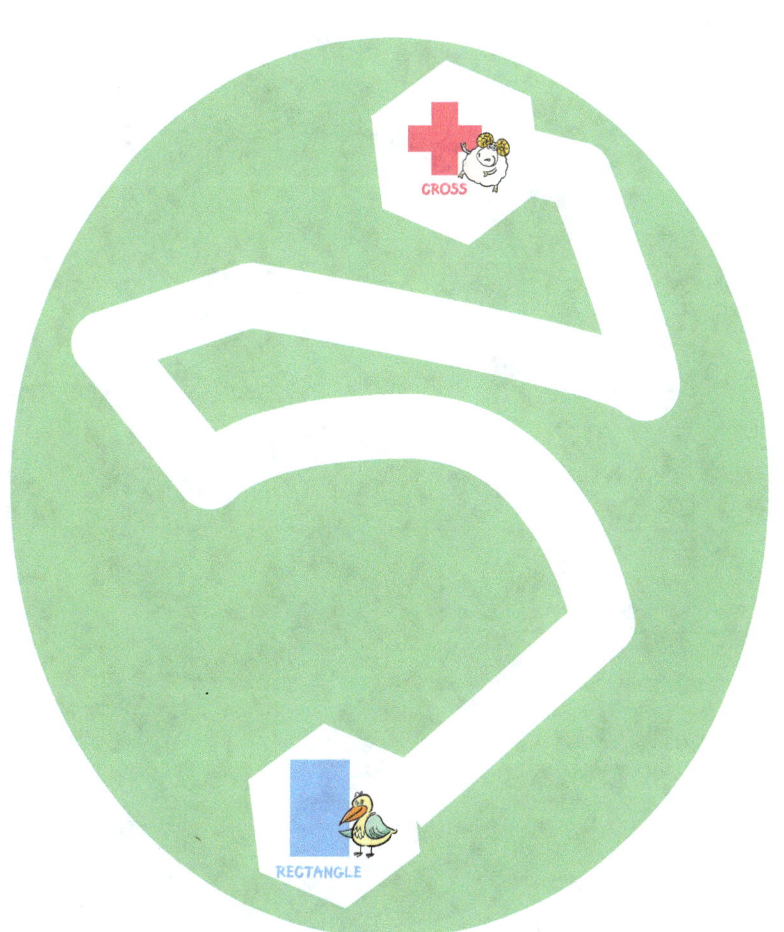

DRAW A LINE TO CONNECT THE SHAPE AND FORM A SHAPE.

DRAW A LINE TO CONNECT THE SHAPE AND FORM A SHAPE.

DRAW A LINE TO CONNECT THE SHAPE AND FORM A SHAPE.

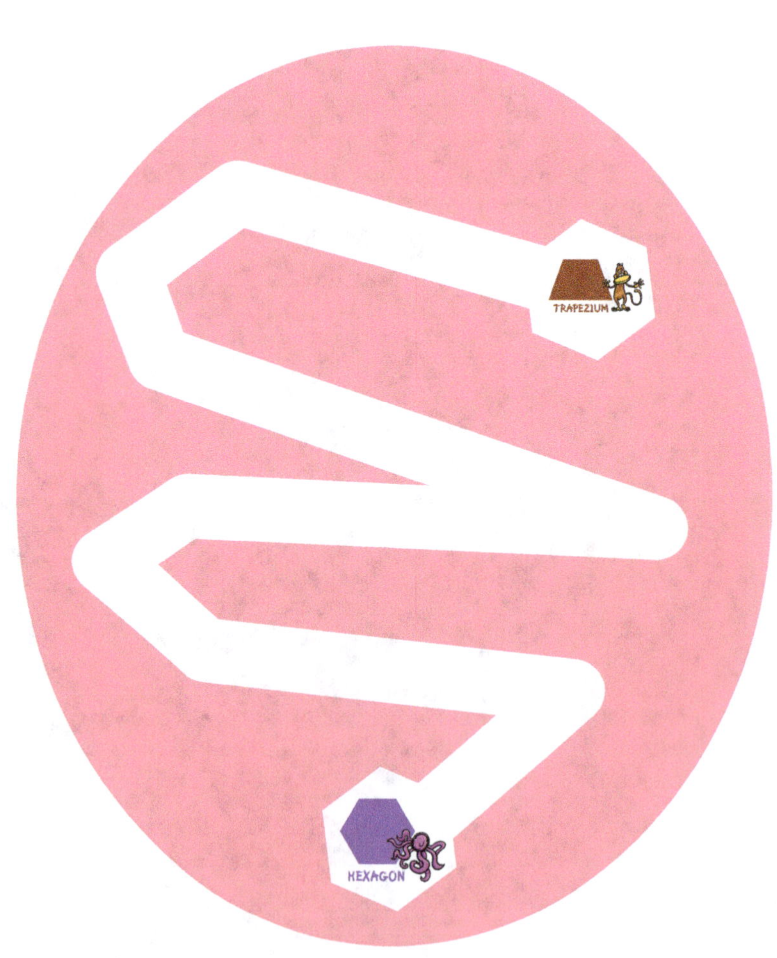

DRAW A LINE TO CONNECT THE SHAPE AND FORM A SHAPE.

DRAW A LINE TO CONNECT THE SHAPE AND FORM A SHAPE.

DRAW A LINE TO CONNECT THE SHAPE AND FORM A SHAPE.

DRAW A LINE TO CONNECT THE SHAPE AND FORM A SHAPE.

DRAW A LINE TO CONNECT THE SHAPE AND FORM A SHAPE.

DRAW A LINE TO CONNECT THE SHAPE AND FORM A SHAPE.

Great Job Kid!
I hope you had fun
doing the activities.

Keep Practicing!

Visit
BABY PROFESSOR
EDUCATION KIDS
www.BabyProfessorBooks.com
to download Free Baby Professor eBooks and view
our catalog of new and exciting Children's Books

www.ingramcontent.com/pod-product-compliance
Lightning Source LLC
Chambersburg PA
CBHW081603120726
47973CB00045B/72

9798869411594